Puss in Boots

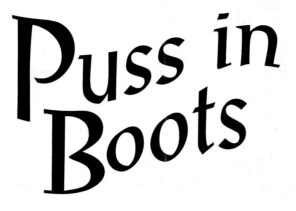

Retold by Fiona Patchett

Illustrated by
Teri Gower

Reading Consultant: Alison Kelly
Roehampton University

Contents

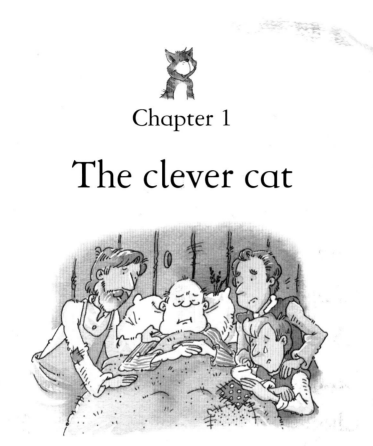

Chapter 1

The clever cat

Once there was a poor miller, who had three sons. When he died, he left them all he had in the world: his mill, his donkey and his orange tabby cat.

3

Before anyone could blink, the eldest son took the mill. Then the middle brother grabbed the donkey. Tom, the youngest, was left with the cat.

He wasn't impressed. "You two can work together and earn a living," Tom grumbled. "What can I do with Puss? Maybe I'll have to eat him!"

Help! I need a plan fast.

Later, when they were alone,
Puss jumped onto Tom's lap.

Don't look so
gloomy, Master.

"Things are not as bad as
they seem," he said, with a
purr. "Find me a bag and a
pair of boots and you'll see."

Tom was astonished. Puss could talk!

I have one amazing cat.

And then Tom remembered that he had often seen Puss using incredibly clever tricks to catch rats and mice.

So, Tom found Puss a leather bag and a shiny pair of boots. He gave him a cloak and a floppy hat too.

The cat filled the bag with carrots and strutted off into the fields.

Chapter 2

Puss goes to work

Puss headed for a field where
he knew there were lots of
rabbits. Opening the bag, he
stretched out on the ground
and pretended to be dead.

Just as he expected, a foolish young rabbit came bouncing along and sniffed the carrots. As it poked its quivering nose into the bag, Puss pounced.

Puss was delighted with
his catch. He marched
straight to the
palace and
asked to see
the king.

In front of the throne, Puss bowed low. "Your Royal Highness, I have brought you a gift from my master, the Duke of Carabas."

How amazing! A talking cat...

"How kind. Thank your master very much," replied the king.

The next day, Puss went into the fields again. This time, he hid among some golden corn. He held his bag wide open...

...and two partridges flew straight in. Puss chuckled as he pulled the drawstring tight.

13

Once more, Puss took his catch to the king.

Take these for your master.

Puss became a regular visitor to the palace. Soon, the king began to wonder who the generous duke was.

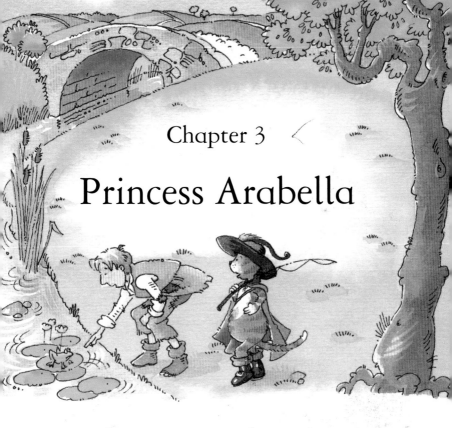

Chapter 3

Princess Arabella

One day, Puss and Tom were walking by the river. Puss knew the king would be driving by with his beautiful daughter, Princess Arabella, and he had a plan.

15

When Puss spotted the royal coach in the distance, he turned to Tom. "Quick! Take off your clothes and jump in the river," he told him.

It's freezing!

Tom was puzzled, but he trusted Puss, so he jumped in.

A minute later, Tom was even more puzzled. First, Puss hid all his clothes under a large stone. Then he started to scream. "Help! Help! Please rescue my master, the Duke of Carabas!"

As the royal coach came by, the king recognized Puss. "Guards! Pull the duke out of the water at once," he ordered.

"Dreadful thieves attacked my master and stole his clothes," Puss explained.

"That's terrible," said the king, "but I think I can help." He snapped his fingers and a servant ran up.

All this time, Princess Arabella had been watching from the coach.

When she saw Tom in his fine, new clothes, she jumped from her seat. He was so handsome.

Tom bent and kissed Princess
Arabella on the hand.

"Oh!" she gasped and smiled.

21

The king insisted that Puss and the duke join them on their drive.

"You go, master," said Puss, pushing Tom forward. "I have some errands to run."

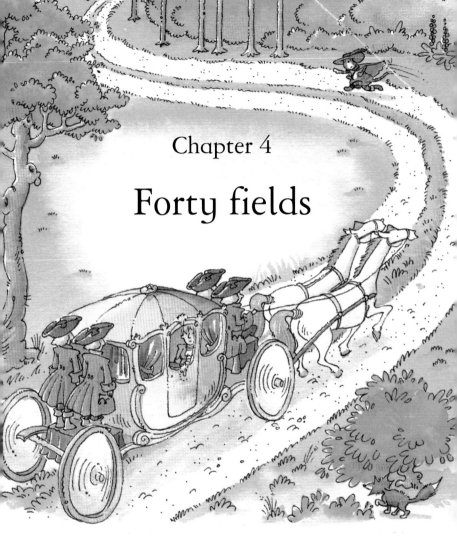

Chapter 4

Forty fields

As the coach rumbled along,
Puss raced ahead. He still
had lots to do.

Before long, he came to some men mowing a field. Puss clapped his paws.

"Listen to me!" he shouted. "When the king drives by, tell him this field belongs to the Duke of Carabas, or my master will chop you into mincemeat!"

A talking cat – his master must be a magician!

The men didn't dare refuse.

Sure enough, when the king arrived, he asked them who owned the field.

The men had been so frightened by Puss's threats, they all spoke together.

Tom was astonished to hear them tell the king this was his land, but he decided to play along.

This field always produces a good harvest.

Puss ran ahead. In the next field he passed, some men were reaping grain.

"Tell the king this field belongs to the Duke of Carabas," he snarled, "or my master will grind you into mincemeat!"

Horrified, the men agreed.

When the royal coach
arrived at the next field, the
king got out. This field was
twice as big as the one before.

"Who owns this field?" he
asked some workers.

"The Duke of Carabas, Your
Highness," they replied.

Puss made the same threat
to everyone he met. The king
was astonished at how much
land the duke owned.

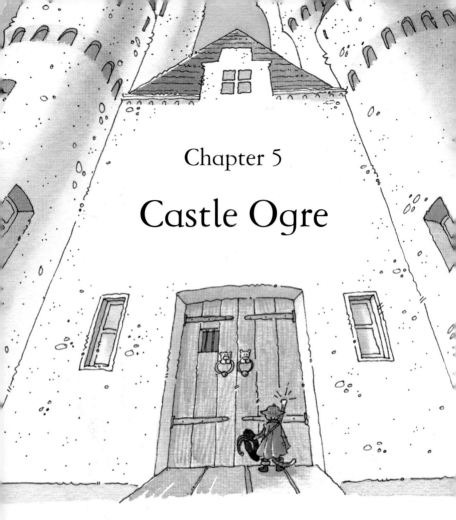

Chapter 5

Castle Ogre

Finally, Puss reached a magnificent castle. It was owned by a fierce ogre, but that didn't stop Puss.

This ogre happened to be one of the richest ogres in the country. All the land they had passed on the way was actually his.

The ogre greeted Puss, licking his lips, and invited the cat inside.

Puss smiled. He was about to try his biggest trick. "I've heard," he said to the ogre, "that you can change yourself into any creature you want. Could you really turn into an elephant or a lion?"

See for yourself!

It was true. In seconds, the
ogre turned into a huge lion.
Puss was terrified.

After growling and roaring for a while, the ogre changed back to himself.

"That was the most frightening thing I've ever seen!" cried Puss.

34

"But I've also been told," he went on, "that you can change into a really small animal, such as a rat or a mouse."

"Of course," said the ogre, rather boastfully.

Isn't that impossible?

Just watch!

And he did! But
as soon as Puss saw
the tiny mouse scampering
around, he leaped on him and
gobbled him up.

36

Chapter 6

A royal wedding

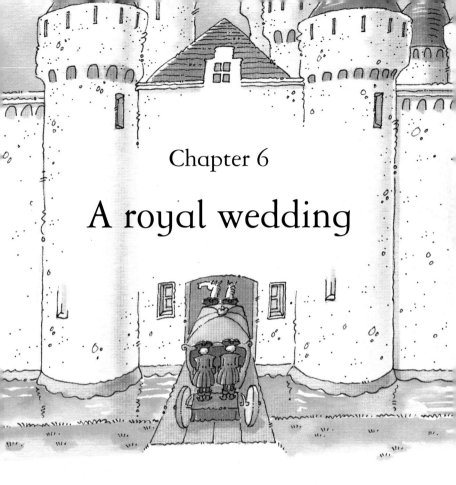

By this time, the royal coach
had reached the ogre's castle.

"Let's visit," said the king,
who wanted to see who owned
such a grand home.

Puss heard the coach clattering over the drawbridge and flung open the castle doors. "Your Majesty, welcome to the castle of my master, the Duke of Carabas."

"You mean you own this splendid castle, as well as all that land?" the king asked Tom in amazement.

Trying to hide his surprise, Tom nodded.

"Would you mind if I took a look around?" asked the king. "Not at all," said Tom.

40

In the banqueting hall, a grand feast had been laid out for the ogre. The table was crammed with pies, meat, cheeses, trifles and cakes.

The king's mouth started to water. "That does look good!" he said.

"Please join us for lunch," said Puss.

The king was impressed
with the duke's wonderful
castle, and Princess Arabella
thought he was kind to let
them share his feast.

As the king ate, he noticed that the duke and his daughter were getting along very well indeed. He realized the duke would make a perfect prince.

By the end of the meal, the king could not keep his thoughts to himself.

"Duke of Carabas," he declared, "will you marry my daughter?"

I'd be delighted, Sire.

A wedding was arranged for the very next day.

And so the miller's youngest son became a prince and lived happily in the castle with his beautiful bride.

Tom's brothers were both made earls. As for Puss, he became a lord and never had to chase mice again...

...except for fun!

47

Puss in Boots is a well-known fairy tale that has been passed from generation to generation by word of mouth. The French writer, Charles Perrault, first wrote it down in 1697. It was one of eight fairy tales he wrote in a book called *Tales of Mother Goose*. The other stories included *Sleeping Beauty*, *Little Red Riding Hood*, *Babes in the Wood*, *Cinderella* and *Tom Thumb*.

Series editor: Lesley Sims
Designed by Russell Punter

First published in 2005 by Usborne Publishing Ltd., Usborne House, 83-85 Saffron Hill, London EC1N 8RT, England. www.usborne.com
Copyright © 2005 Usborne Publishing Ltd.